Kristen Noelle Richards

THE DESERT IS A WOMAN TOO

A Poetry Collection

Indie Earth Publishing Inc.
| Miami, FL |

INDIE EARTH
PUBLISHING

Advance Praise for
THE DESERT IS A WOMAN TOO

"Kristen Richards' *The Desert is a Woman Too* takes the reader on a lyrical journey through the soul of a woman inextricably bound to the natural world. Vivid imagery paints landscapes of rippled desert sands, sun-dappled forest pines, and star-strewn skies, all mirroring the depths of her own spirit. Each poem whispers a resonating message, weaving a tapestry of resilience, growth, and the profound connection between a woman and the wild earth that sustains her. *The Desert is a Woman Too* is an intimate conversation with nature, a celebration of its beauty, and a call to listen to the wilderness that guides us all."
— AZURE HALL, Author of *Reflections: A Mythology in Poetry & Prose*

"Richards' poetry captivates you. Her written words roll off of the tongue perfectly. I feel like I was a part of the world Richards wanted me to experience."
— AMELIE HONEYSUCKLE, Author of *To Kiss The Lips Of The Maple Tree* and *What Once Was An Inside Out Rainbow*

"*The Desert is a Woman Too* is one of the best poetry collections of 2024! It is brilliant, lyrical, and presents a rich perspective on life, self-love, and the healing energy of nature. Kristen does it once again, blending beautiful prose with what it means to experience the inevitable beauty and hardship of the human condition."
— FLOR ANA, Author of *The Truth About Love* and *A Moth Fell In Love With The Moon*

"Richards' *The Desert is a Woman Too* will make you feel as if you are on a long road trip where nostalgia comes as a gentle reminder to take a glance at where we are, at how far we have come, and to continue despite how long the roads may be."
— FIN ROSE ABORIZK, Author of *On the Ever-Lovely Morrow* and *At The Beginning Of Yesterday*

"*The Desert is a Woman Too* is a beautiful unraveling of experience and admiration. Kristen has a gorgeous view of life and the adventures it brings. To experience growth and the feeling of grounding all at once is conveyed brilliantly. I find myself loving the desert as much as her, through her storytelling."
— KENDALL HOPE, Author of *The Willow Weepings* and *Pockets of Lavender*

"*The Desert is a Woman Too* is an elemental blend of vivid imagery, rhythmic language, and personal themes. I found myself reading passages multiple times to hold onto the scenes that came like magic in my mind. My tongue regularly hit the roof of my mouth as the bounce of words inspired my lips to form them as I read. My actual settings vanished before me as I was swept along with each poem showing me something new and gorgeous and intimate. This book isn't one to simply read. It is a collection of small journeys you will return to again and again."
— CHARLES MCCASKILL, Author of *Where I've Laid My Head*

"As I felt with *as if to return myself to the sea*, Kristen's words are very real and thump away at my heart as I read them. *The Desert is a Woman Too* experiments with form more than its predecessor, but the words, emotions, and beautiful imagery all shine just as brightly. This book is a great leap forward and a fantastic addition to any poetry lover's collection"
— MATT NICKLES, Author of *Sooner Than Forever* and *We Were Fire in the Night*

The Desert is a Woman Too

a poetry collection

Kristen Noelle Richards

contents

SUNRISE... 1

contents

SOLAR NOON... 31

contents

GOLDEN HOUR... 57

contents

SUNSET... 93

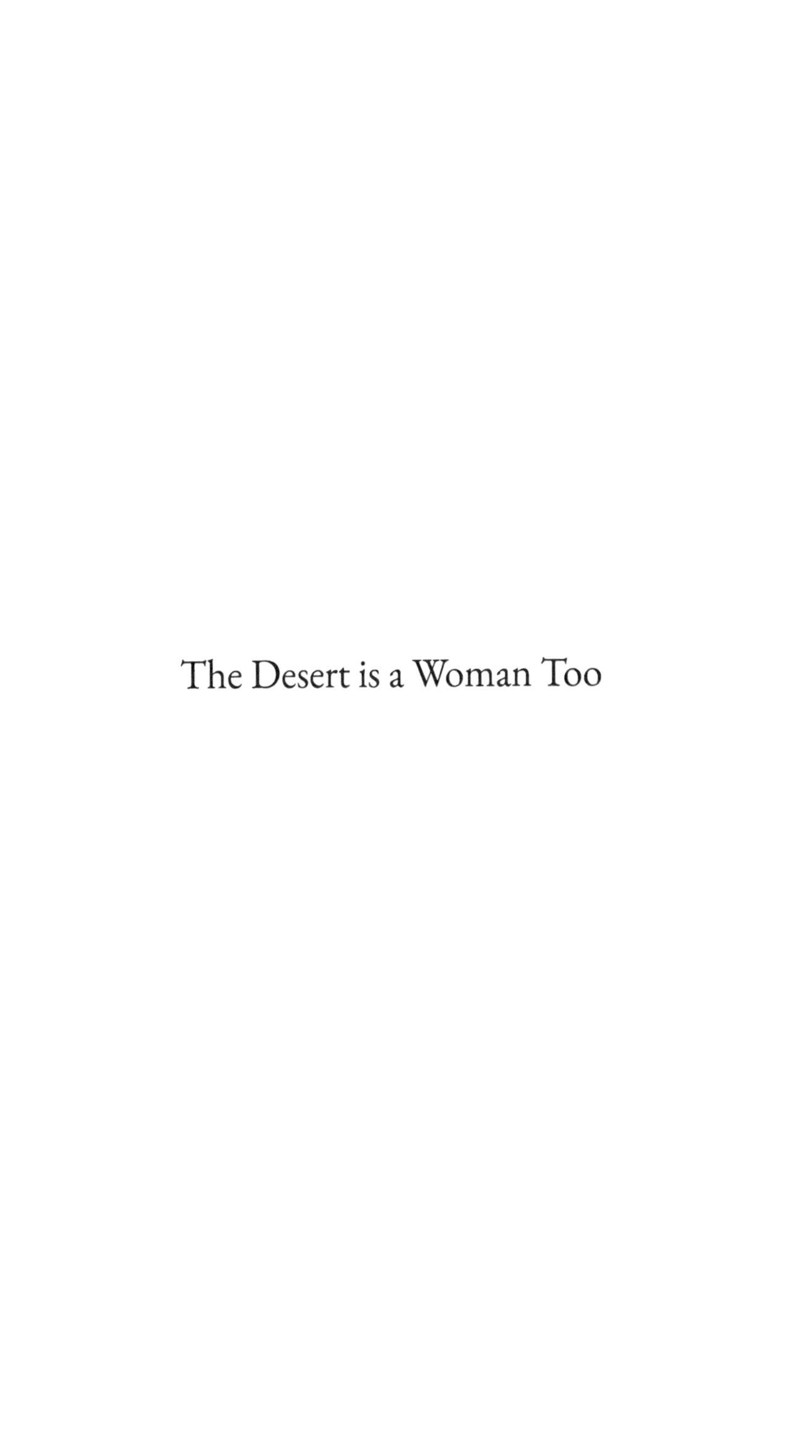

The Desert is a Woman Too

for everyone who has fallen in love with the desert,
even if just for a moment

"You do not have to walk on your knees
for a hundred miles through the desert repenting.
You only have to let the soft animal of your body love what it loves.
Tell me about despair, yours, and I will tell you mine.
Meanwhile, the world goes on."

- Mary Oliver, "Wild Geese"

~

"It is no measure of good health
to be well adjusted to a sick society."

Andrea Gibson, "The Nutritionist"

sunrise

rebirth and awakening

GIRL GROWTH

girl growth looks like bangs in eyes
shifting slowly, then all. at. once. the sun is
dragging out the growing to nurture the awe.

> *we will keep this cycle as long as the moon*
> *asks us to,*
> *control is futile because, girl,*
> *you have nature on your side.*

and with the sudden jolt of waking from a dream —

i run my fingers through the stones
until i find a way to love the curve;

> *this body is a riverbed of pebbles, always leaving me*
> *thirsty, thinking...*

> *what could we be if we tried for this comfort*
> *one more time.*

girl growth looks like learning
to love the body not just in theory,
but with pleasure
that terrifies all the skin
still stuck in childhood.

she will catch up
and until then,

all the newborn bones will fall asleep
sickened by the *joy* that they look different every day.

to find this much pride in change means
flowing boundless through seasons, saying:
in the summer
i count my freckles
to see how many times
the sun has kissed me today

girl growth is the fascination with fear

                              how could i *possibly* feel this much unease

by my own being?
                              and how she chooses to shape herself –

remember, the moon has offered to care for the molding,
and the girl growth comes in the   belief and
                                                         knowing

my body will be alright. yet,

                              girl growth is monetized and measured,
                                 by all the cages i strap my body into
                                    at the beginning of each day.

                                                 for to have a fold
out of place is to call nude a disgrace, bound the body
like it was meant to be
 a cookie dough form
baked too long,
crusted over the paper
and stuck to the edges
of its own home. naked
is beautiful, and
when you say it is not

i swear i will hold on that much harder to love.

no, there is a moment when girl growth could become
what the moon has promised it would not have to be,
and for years, these moments collect as birthday wishes
spent   not   on   shrinking,

but

                                                            blossoming.

there is nothing
more understood
 than your body by the earth, so

let it be. remember: *the desert is a woman too.*

DAYDREAMS

daydreams of strawberry soil
ripe from love's tongue and tingling

a dandelion bulb in still air while
summer rocks its body:

we are all widened by snowmelt.

~~

daydreams for the underbellies
of sea sticks, silent as balloon clouds

coiling around the middle finger of august
finding beads of sunlight in the exit wound.

~~

daydreams for the dry creek bed,
tearless and mourning, lullaby is a verb

tightening around the trunk of every tree
calling for someone to stay.

~~

daydreams of licorice twists and candle wax,
heat burned cold straight from the ember,

the crown builds around an orange flame,
all the places where sugar stretches it thin.

~~

daydreams with the old, yellowed eyes
of a tabby cat, the knitting together
of a spider's web over a metal stove

living in the lives we leave behind.

~~

imagine throwing water at a problem
like this:

kindling burnt top down
like it was meant to be stone

all along i knew i was fire
but you wouldn't let me stay,

said *you can't always be flame
girl, you will burn out,
if you work that hard with
no one else's help*

THE WAY EVERYTHING IS SUPPOSED TO GO

when the colorado river turned brown
i split the canyon in half just to find:

snow in my socks   and
hope in the fire

when every bone in me screamed *!!desert!!*
it snowed 12ft on the north rim of the grand canyon
and i skinned my knee in the parking lot,
hands greasy with motor oil.

the way everything is supposed to go
is the last way it will ever be.

earth will dare
for a snowstorm in may,
for a flat tire,
for drying pine needles to be carried home
by the bottom of my shoes

so the next time you think
you drove 10 hours for *that*,
for half a mile and ripped leggings,
for $75 worth of gas,

i will say *yes!*

10 hours is not a lot if you have spent
10 years running
when the earth offers me her curves
i will always say **yes**.
i am here for just the view

for just the breath, to open
my car windows when i cross the colorado border
and try to breathe the canyon
into something true.

RIVER SONG (PART 1)

the beat of the river is salt
black rock slick body driving
forward,
every night arrives
in a new place. this smoke is

wanting to be flame,   i am
wanting to be fire,   dancing

the river song, my edges curved
and heavy, drawn in sand
the memories that remain
are crystals, are crusted,
encapsulated by the sea.

what if
i let you run through me
exactly as you long to do, let go
of where i have always wished to be
hands clamped on the idea
of growing up.

this river song
is an evolution, a folding of age,

i never knew water could be
this.

WHAT I DON'T BELIEVE IN
CAN STILL BECOME ME

you look like sunlight, she tells me
like summer mornings. i am still
in my own skin, the unbecoming
caught in the back of my throat.

for all of june i will curdle myself
around arizona's relentless dust and breathe
my body to reality. we are watching
the desert for signs of weakness
and it gives us none. my feet become stronger
barefoot and wild and fearless
for cacti, for rain, for dusk to settle
over heat and wonder: *what does it look like
to be the moon?* this, i would give it all up
to be.

sometimes *it is just the imagining,*
i tell her. *what i don't believe in
can still become me.* these are
conversations of the crust, dictionary
dancing for words
and all the phrases i will never dare to say.
to be me, she says, *is to light the moon.*

she is the sun.

LETTER TO SELF-LOVE

(((one)))

this morning, i am thinking
through my body, the heart's laugh
and the chest hum: *i* am my own song
and i let the melody become
rhythm in the desert.

my god, the tongue is crying,
we have not had a single thought all day
      we are cozy in the quiet, don't bring
         in the telephone wires or mirrors;
            our reflection is not something
              we can unpeel,
      like paint layers on skin
this kindness is calm in the canyon

<u>this</u> is a letter to self-love, all the verses
the choir can sing blind,
        the body
        is more present than it has ever been
        print out the paper, sign it, divorce
        the things that do not matter

(((two)))

the cause for believing
is not seeing, but <u>feeling</u>

i can write more than i can know.

my body is poetry lines that need no editing
i cannot say this enough
to you: all the courage
                                 and all the living,
                                 you do not have to

define it to do it;   i have been
                                 waking to words
                                 i do not know

the meaning to, the unlearning
is okay if you know <u>compassion</u>
and the way it looks at your smile
like it is the most wonderful thing
ever offered to the world,

your joy alone can be called
 the wind.

girl, this is the unbecoming
and the world wants you to be joy itself.

(((three)))

i am left alone with my body
and it saying *finally, finally*
                          your arguments are fairytales
and your words are sweet, like
fresh mango slippery from its skin
say **no** to the trauma,

                   do not let it
                   see all of you;

your life is so much more
than this grief for your smaller self

(((four)))
your body deserves to be kind
to the parts of you it does not know
yet. there are no rules to this religion –

i am not crawling through the desert
with a long line of people who want saving,
                   you are the saving.
                   <u>the body</u> is the saving,
and now,   the morning is ending.

(((five)))

the sun dips beneath the horizon,
holding its breath under the surface;
the eyes are asking to be closed.
i never learned how to pray, but my body knows
how to say *thank you* to the sky,
thank you to the shadow
and the shade,
             and the warm rocks
against my back in the nighttime

SKY IN MY BONES

see, i was born with the sky in my bones
and a little fear of the rain; i was bound
to become like this: reckless abandon for joy
giving up the comfort for the love.
it hurts to feel this solace. you were taught
to hold on to wind and let it carry you west
–a methodical choice for the uncontrollable–
there is no part of me that thinks
you are anything less than the sun.

01833

the cookbooks in the small town library remind me
of the warmth in my mother's kitchen, way back to 2008,
when simplicity still split right down the middle,
shaken into good and bad. rotten apples were easy
to throw out; there was not enough
at stake those years.

reading cookbooks is telling myself to boil,
how to let blood reach the point where it can
make something really cook and truly change;
i am surrounded by the people who have time
to mince garlic with a butter knife and dice onions
until they disintegrate in just a drop of olive oil.

pressing my body against the page, i desire something
different. i am wishing to be the kind of person
who isn't afraid of the sweetness of lemon curd
and whose lullaby will one day become the insistent hum
of a stand-alone mixer at its softest speed.

LEARNING TO READ A COMPASS

somewhere along I-70 there's a 2005 honda accord
with northern arizona dirt stuck in snow-chained tires.
spit me out onto the freeway, i found one road
and it only leads west. turn the cold upside down, build
the land around the city and watch the heat waves burn.

i left a wet bathing suit in the backseat for the whole summer
until i hit the colorado border and realized i didn't want it anymore,
couldn't want it anymore, not the nylon or the polyester,
not what it felt like to breathe when my body was inside it.
so i left it in the trash can outside the gas station
and called my mother, still a two-days drive away.
i never wanted anything when she was close,
only distance asked me to be her daughter.

when all i could see was sky behind burnt-out headlights,
i scraped my naked toe against the underbelly of my car.
then realized i had no band-aids, watched as the pharmacies
along the road changed shape and name,
but the brands inside stayed the same, so i told myself it was okay
to call this place home too.

waking up already with regret, washing my socks
in the river outside moab, wishing away the rain
that wasn't going to be there anyway. i hung wet clothes
on the side mirror and drove down the highway, watching the wind
dry them, and a few hours outside sedona, i was still looking
for a black bean burger and a cup of lemonade, something
to keep my stomach stretched like mountain towns
all along the same line. i woke up knowing
that today was going to be one alone
and wanting it to be; solitary minds are easy

to compromise with.

the cold apple juice that comes in the glass bottle, the one
you can only find in a gas station outside flagstaff, that is
what i drive on for, some days. like maybe the leaving
is all to make staying
feel better.

and when the wheels cannot be pointed any way but east,
sleep through missouri, a campground where i find
a tiny blue scorpion crawling on my tent, a picnic table
sticky from last season's s'mores. the humidity of iowa so putrid
it smells like a dirty fishtank left out in the sun. when i start
to recognize town names, whatever song i am listening to
sounds like the ocean,
sounds like the white noise machine i couldn't buy
in the flyover states. this sound stolen
from the place where the sounds came from. and crossing
the massachusetts border, the gas tank never drops below full.

THE FIRST CAMPFIRE IN SEDONA

the first campfire in sedona
was in a dirty metal cage of a firepit
and the smoke seemed to fall apart
before hitting my glassy eyes.
ash and hands. dirt on pants. socks.
the family the next campsite over
had a pit piled thick with kindling
a bright orange flame with no smoke.
but fire doesn't count until the sun goes down
drunk desire only hides heat in the dark.
beyond us all, the smell of burning sage
aches, taunts, and
there are so many words i rush to say aloud
i am in love with my ability to do this
climb down on earth's roof to start
a flame no one knows will last, and after
the first rainshower, i am tough
in my backseat, crying.

THIS MORNING

this morning i am socks in sandals
stale bagels and cowboy coffee
cold fingers and a rising sun

WINTER IN NEW HAMPSHIRE

maple syrup in gallon jugs on the mantle
a fire screaming to die but laughing itself back to life
this winter is like the first footprints in fresh snow.

i am ripping through backcountry roads
like i was born to read their every line, every day
this sky smiles the same – barely even a grimace.

waking to sore bones in a boarding school bed,
the morning i call for a translation from the dreamscape,
where the sun also rises is the closest this life will ever be to beautiful.

I HAVE BEEN OUT CAMPING

i have been out camping
> is my favorite excuse.
> it means

i cannot respond because i'm watching the river
> and

i probably won't call you back today, but

i will still think of you, constantly.

SKID

she asks me

do you have to know
what you are
writing about?

it is the night she smells of lemongrass,
fills up my whole being with frothy love,

i tell her it is all
but my subconscious
that ties the ribbon
of my heart to the pen,
to her –

grasshoppers in the garden
this farmhouse is glassy with
butter on toast
maple syrup on pancakes
coffee, just brewed

we wrap yesterday in a

sphere,

skid into the driveway fast
to catch the sunrise.

WHAT THE DIRT IN ME FEARS

friday nights in a city i've never been to before yesterday, i am more
scared of the way the half-hearted billboards reflect in pavement puddles

than where i am going when the sun rises. this city is a costume
or a skin i must shed. i am finding the places i don't belong to,

which corners will lead back to themselves; i swear every map i find
is always telling me to *go back to the desert,*
                                   back to no water and no lights –

i know what it is like to sit in the dark and write
                                   on paper i cannot even see
yet i do not know what to do with myself beneath
                                   a bus stop awning or

whose conversation to listen to in a busy cafe. i am wondering what
these people are wondering, *what's behind your computer screen,*
                                   in your notebook?

what book are you trying to sew yourself into, where does the story lead
as you close the last page? somehow i saw myself here, maybe at a time

it was rainy in colorado too, i thought there would be
a sort of familiarity in sidewalk curb puddles,
in the bookstore shelves, in fresh espresso and steamed milk.

there is not always an overlap, i am learning,
 in experiences that once drew similarity in themselves

but this city might prove me a writer more than the desert can claim
and that is what the dirt in me fears.

PLEASE CONSIDER THE FOLLOWING

please consider the following for publication: i am
promising my own wonder to be something
born out of the unpopped kernels, of   heat
that radiates and threatens to undo
all that has been done and grown,   everything
                                                    i have been saving
                                                              to say

until my words can travel a little bit farther, maybe even touch
themselves, circle back to their own sound,
swallow their clusters and curls of lips, windowless
and daring to be shared.

please consider the following for publication:
                                                    it is

my own blood, water, soil and roots, my own
springtime, what becomes of the unbecoming,
                                                    i am at last
defined by the words i write, wrote. perhaps, i am wishing
to be justified, for someone to say i see you too and
                                                    i want to
hear all of what has been ripped you from you,

what has not been seen
is what needs to be shown today,

                                        retrace the roadmap of trauma
and make yourself young, learn to be a child again
through words. someone told me once
that rejection is what makes you a writer, if only i could accept
 identity as defined by what i cannot do.

THE CAROUSEL

a carnival at dusk, where

just with the listless sky

you can see the tongues of the buried
etched in hot sand

a coin flip on the beach,
the end of this always swells to sea

then: the summer of your voice over laminated seawater

- *tell me the story again.*

THE PROMISE OF PROSE

Prose promises to make sense out of the wonder, the fear. The extra words give me time to think and remember that I cannot break up the lines just because I feel the discomfort when they touch. They are always touching, running and breaking only when they have to. These words find the beauty in conforming.

IN THE BACKSEAT OF YESTERDAY'S CAR

all that i don't belong to is wild
each day i spent thinking the memory clear
doing all i could to not let it go
but 5 years passed and it is all blurred
to outlines, to vague feelings,
moments of stopping in the forest, saying
                    i remember this smell from that summer
sun dancing on ponderosa pine
the itching of dirt under my fingernails
remembering what it felt like to breathe
something real, to feel
yesterday's ghost in every sunset
and cry it back to its mother, i am
bread tags on the rim of a sunhat,
the feeling of being trapped has never felt so comforting
as now i have learned to love the letting go
of control. after all, it is relief that is rigid.

I DREAM TO MAKE FLOWERS FROM THIS

my grandmother's garden grows with the seasons
and when spring comes, the day lilies wake, and
i have never seen so much life than i have
in watching her watch the flowers bloom. how many years
have you stood at the kitchen window waiting for the winter
to paint itself pink and green? i have always seen
the blossoming happen slowly, then all at once

one day, i wake up and all the world
is purple.

i am starting to understand the need to beautify in this way,
to absorb nature with itself. planting these flowers
is believing the earth can mother itself;
it wasn't until i had a yard i called my own
that i saw this dirt as a place where flowers could grow

perhaps this is all just a 500-sq ft backyard, but i will take it
for every penny, i will stretch each inch and learn to love
every twist and grizzle.

solar noon

authenticity and vitality

THE DESERT IS A WOMAN TOO

each day more silent
more green, more willing.
bodies made of sand
sitting themselves upon red dirt
rock faces and curved edges
the desert is a woman too.

THE WANT IS THE WILLING

it was the year i told myself, foolishly,

i am not going to do anything that does not bring me joy

before i chose the night shift
hours of dishes and when i came home
i couldn't do my own.

the joy does not come from a paycheck
i don't need this, this
stability. it does not exist. it is
something i thought i had before
i forgot the year i told myself, foolishly,

i am not going to do anything that does not bring me joy

days like this stretch out long under the sun
evening holds itself back
for so long i follow doubt to the windowsills
and wonder if the sun will ever go to bed.

these are the moments that texture is the breath
of every word i have written, texture is
my movement and my stillness, texture is
the long way home.

OUT OF SORTS

dry legs from river salt
sitting in the shade of the car
toasting our escape from the heat   with

lukewarm capri sun juice boxes
these are the days we are filling ourselves   with

what in childhood we could not have.

growing old is not to learn
it is to remember
what it felt like to first wake up.

ONLY DEAD FISH SWIM WITH THE CURRENT

i don't want to go back to you.
only dead fish swim with the current
and i am screaming my way upstream,
desperately doubting the odds,
shifting probability to a new time zone

this only has to be as hard as you make it.

my weight is calculated by my measurement
of connection with the ground, leaves and rocks.
love this process of dedication,
growing smaller to be closer to the woman
arm of nature who made me. but no

we are not meant to return from the wonder
retract the tidal waves of our bodies;
we are meant to be fire in the night,
loving the flame.

SUNNY DISPOSITION

i am so terrified for these words to be real
i write them with an eraser clenched in one hand:
my third grade cursive.

someone asked me once

[how can you choose this, day after day?]

and later i spoke to myself with more fear
than i had felt in months:

[how do i know i *am* doing this, day after day?]

THE EXCEPTION

syllables like socks
like the hard metal handle of a   wheelbarrow at   dusk
like a   triple folded paper note   saying
                      i'll be home by 6

words in greeting and goodbyes,
the pictures in between:
           we are nothing if not vain.

a wildflower reenactment,
            i live to smell the trees
like ponderosa pines and juniper
        playing the part of dirt,
        i am always
searching for steadier ground.

dialing the landline to a number
that always loops back to itself, stuck
in a cycle of wash and dry but never clean
satisfaction looks like tires deep in mud,
the unrequited effort of trying to get out, to resist
pushing against fate like a broken lock,
a numberless keypad, towels over skin in the rain
we do what is futile over and over
wanting to be the exception.

i probably won't be home by six because
i am trying to find cause and meaning
in what for years i have been told is
unnecessary.

SANDPAPER BUTTONS

sandpaper buttons on last year's sweater
my fingers are trying to find
the place where the fabric breaks –

                                 – i am waiting for sea glass
                                         to slice me out.

                it is the new moon,
the dark sky still stringy with clouds, brilliant
with the pops of an open flame
in cooling desert air. all i am sure of
is how it will feel to wake
with the country growing warm.

                                        each hour

experiences in utah form in my mind
convincing me that i can be fully in
a place for a single day

this type of traveling is the reason
                    i don't need to believe every new town can be my home.

WHY I CHOSE YOU (PART 1)

because i loved you more than i craved running
and your eyes were more like home than the feeling of being empty
i dare myself to shape my life around you. see
it had always been just me and my bones; it was safer
because i could be my own lamplight. what is means
to be a writer and fall in love is to give my words
to the lonely side of a sage bush leaf, let you see
how the ground loves to feel the earth and teach you
all the nuances of my language.

SHEETS

you say
when we live together we will wash the sheets every week,
we will make beauty from this mess.
i will find home in your eyes.

LAVENDER, MINT, HONEY

cozy
is hot breath in cold air
wrapping the feeling of warmth
around cups over camp stoves
all the places we let the river
run through.

i am learning to love the wet,
the indescribable, what makes
the green flow so vibrantly. the sun
is waiting for the rain
so it can rest.

redefining the comfortable is
driving myself awake on a foggy night
goosebumps are not just for fear
they are to show me i'm alive.

look at my skin, it is the reaction to self

in another town there would be beauty
in sheets, hot water thrown
over cold skin, soap that runs
from my fingertips to the drain
disappears leaving lavender, mint, honey

four pillows too many. sunlight waking me
with curtain left undrawn, a morning
where i can't hear the bird song
but i know it is there.

THE DAY I QUIT MY JOB AS A BARISTA

the day i quit my job as a barista
i said,
*maybe money is more a current
than a currency, it is meant
to flow through and don't let it
ever get comfortable enough to stay.*

i promise it is a privilege
for my cereal box dollar bills to think
themselves even close to the nothingness
i am letting them be. i want them
to see me as stains on the sidewalk
wild only when wettened, where all the coins
in the claw machine drop cold and hard
against metal.

the day i quit my job as a barista
i threw out this odd green apron
and washed the coffee out of every smell
there is *more* to this life than being caffeinated
and counting the hours to sundown.

THE LAVENDER HANGOVER

the lavender hangover:
from the sidewalk smells of downtown,
here is the boomerang of the pollen that becomes me

we are coughing and laughing, bellies grumbling –
we are waving our goodbyes to the crosswalk man.

i usually would say i am pansy petals in dust,
but in these city lights, i am sterile sunflower
three shades too bright to not be the sun. as always,

i am dreaming this to be a small town legend, like the place
i am from.

you listen to the birds' song as we wander, the scrunchy of time
tight around eager beaks approaching lunchtime.

imagine this: these city streets and lavender growing so wild
it is in my every breath.

ACADEMIC (DIS)HONESTY

the truth i've found in school buildings is
they are built on the courage to ignore.

today i wake up to realize:
i am afraid this school will run the wild out of me

                                                and

                here

i do not fit in because i do not want my life
to be a long stretch of
                    i know what happens next

THE DAY AFTER I QUIT MY JOB AS A BARISTA

i stayed up to watch the stars and
counted them on my hands
like freckles on my body, an itinerary for the want.

it was a calculation of possession
what i could see became mine

and i had the ability to give it all up
and still ask for more.

UTAH

it is time
to watch the cars
pull away
from the shoreline.
the cliffs see
their retreat,
attempt to fit
everything
in the trunk
of a subaru –
close myself in
away from desert
and moon,
leap straight from
day to day,
wish for reality
to only feel
like comfort, to
never really see
this desert
for what it is.

WHY I CHOSE YOU (PART 2)

beauty comes to me in waves
the bedrock of the ocean
in this desert
is a leaf drawn sideways
and wandering towards the sun.
you remember the stars on the back edges
of lighthouses off the coast
and shadows of mountains
on the moon; i remember
mornings, rising the sun
myself and watching you wake.
it is the most beautiful thing
i have seen all summer,
more than red rocks
upside down and smiling.
you see the world
and it is new. every year
has no calendar edges, just
june repeating itself, the
almost disintegrating spring
and wettening of summer, august
and october, kissing fall
slowly. seasons are beautiful
in the way they change,
flow effortlessly into one another
with no desire to pause.
with you, i have no desire
to pause.

TRUST

adventure is the word of love
fate can *never* catch up to

DEVIL'S BRIDGE

i do not want to wait in line
to take a photo to prove i was here.
i know i was here. i'll remember it
in the words i wrote about it.

my body bleeds part of the landscape, so much
i dare not etch it to elsewhere. to
outline each curve with the neck of the sky
i'll take a picture
of someone else's photo album, dream myself
to another life where i am not alone, or at the very least,
i do not want to be alone.

but the contentment in my solitary
reminds me to the love the place between
the being and the living. there is so much left
to discover. today i
want to be awake.

DEFINITIONS

i know the definitions of things
i have never had to define, easily.
i can do it as long as you
don't ask me to show you: in theory
we are all our best selves, every day.

SKYLIGHTS

you made these skylights yourself

painting murals of stars
on the ceiling of our tent

with just your words, you
helped me believe
there was more to see

FIFTY-THREE

fifty-three pages of writing
and i have not discovered
a single new thing
about myself. in fact,
i know less about the world
than i did before these words
were written. every day
i am unraveling what it means
to know less, and living wildly in it;
you can still be brave in oblivion.

BOOKENDED BY

w a t e r b u g s,
        on harsh hot rock faces
        northern shade &
sunburn.

property line
fence
     in knee deep river water

          swimming
      w e s t.
    shoreline
    sand
    bellies,
       bags
         left in
       grass,
    chocolate
melting
around
itself.
          laughter
            echoing
              hard
            against
          canyon
       walls,
    these
rocks
    will
       always
    smile,

the desert is a woman too

back
        to
                my
                        wonder.

HALFWAY TO GOODNESS

it is the halfway point and
i have already turned around
asked for someone to lift me
from the bones of the sea and
the burrowing heat of an april desert
because i need to be ready
to hold your hand when it is there,
finally.

golden hour

THE EXPOSITION

part 1: the excellence

writing is the way to say truth
when your mouth cannot collect words
some lips are chapped shut and starving
for lovely breath; mine are
singing a whole town's melody
for the ability to stay closed.

an envelope pushed across a desk on payday,   *please sign*
the pages of a notebook in new hands,
words in sloppy cursive, too mangled
to read, there are

places where a pen can be louder
than the groan of an engine or the screech
and clash of tires, together. if i could not
write my way through these deserts
i would have become so unrooted
as to turn to stone.

part 2: the invitation

today these words are not ready
to be released, the best thing with this way
of communication is the control of the syllables.
no one will hear me stutter, know
the parts of this that were harder to write. you are merely
seeing articles and letters: why do you think
we all assume this means the same thing?
for me, now, every line comes in waves,
and i can choose where it ends, but there
always lies the feeling; my pen runs
out of ink before i realize my heart is dry of love.

part 3: the violation

the man who smashed my window
reached into my words, made me spaghetti
that slipped off the spoon, gum melted
but left unchewed, old sneakers
in a new trash can. he made every cliche
broken at the seams, daring me to use them,
then taunting me for not
inventing the phrases themselves.

my words from arizona were gone;,
i only remembered them, and the way
i wrote them scattered across the page,
in pieces. there are words to that journal
i will spent years trying to rewrite.

the cops sent me the pre-written letter
informing me the case was closed, `things like this`
`happen all the time to everybody and`
`we can't catch who does it. this is life.`

i thought i had the ownership
to bury the poetry where i wanted,
but there was more than just the loss
of words and lines and scrawled letters
from long roadtrips. these were not mine
and i only lost them because i thought
they were.

someone is still out there reading my words.

part 4: the belonging

the first time i wrote to the rim
i danced circles and dug
until night pushed me to sleep and
brought me to day. every thought
of who i was had been documented
in love letters to the sea,
couplets about mountains, and long lists
of things i feared for in the desert.
my solitary became my conscience.
i wrote what i wrote because there was
no one telling me i should have
done it differently. it was real and
i was terrified: listless and direct
pen movements would never be the same.

in the woods this time, i invited
the canyons, the flowers, the wind.
i let the outside be a melody
not the song, giving just enough
life to keep the inspiration breathing

and i also found you

the proximity of my notebook pages
to someone i love is far enough away
that my need for her
and my need for writing
can sometimes try to touch.

so this time, instead of running
from the rim with long lines and
dozens of notebook pages sailing

towards sky, instead of keeping everything
closed until it absolutely has to be
opened, i will let her eyes be mine
and unread the words i have written
        often but never said.

TARANTULA HUNTING AT DUSK

dirt settles under heavy tires, the horizon
defined and dark
against a setting sun.

i am looking for what i do not want
to find; i want the hot noon
back, the ache and echo of
voices over canyon walls, every city
noise and vocal cord, broken from screaming–

i think that maybe if i could see it
i would fear it less, if i could hold
the haunting in my hands and let it
do all it could to hurt me and still
both of us, live.

tonight's sunset is a splintered breath,
the beauty of the pale blue twilight and
the lingering yellow; my fingers follow
the dirt as it darkens.

i retreat knowing your presence
is longing to be alone, i am scaring myself
out of fear. here, in this desert, i am searching
for all that i do not want to find.

FEAR

i wish the fear was in the *forgetting*
not in **memory** chasing me down
another *canyon*, right before

the sun sets.

CRYSTALS

this step west of reality, i offer to you
an afternoon in the coffee and crystal shop
on the outskirts of sedona, red rocks,

here is where curiosity and imagination embrace,
here is the only place

                                           i have ever been sure
faith is like wildflowers, grows beyond where it has been planted

these petals full of doubt, they live on
not knowing the joy the sun and rain offer, combined,
the water just comes when it is time

                          and sometimes
                          that is too late.

faith cannot always be heat,
like me, it will melt back to childhood
and forget how to walk on two feet, only four.

i need a new name for trust,
        a new definition,
                religion
                is nothing if not the violent assertion of truth

but faith is the lack of knowledge, all the things
you cannot prove.
band-aid me over the back pew, i find faith in my feet
and where they take me. every sunday
i say this to myself, a whisper across the desert.

                         and then,

a car window, shattered. missing
wallet, passport, ID. no money, no crime

no money, no crime
no money, no crime.

fraud is shaky and never ending – you tell me.
this paper trail leads back to my front door
bore my hatred for the ambiguity and all the safety
that was lost, all this terror makes me
want to go home,

not here but my real home
                the place i was born,
                the house where i was raised
there is safety in the certain,
even if the certain is not safe.

and there is was: the home i had built for myself
sunburnt in credit card charges
and bank withdrawals,

                i have never let anyone touch me like this
the intimacy is everything but physical
                they can see me, will not stop looking

until my bones are hollow birds,
                retreating to the trees.

i fix my window and mail myself
a new driver's license.
cancel my credit cards.
withdraw just enough cash
to pay for my morning coffee

my lease does not end for three and a half months
but i have already started collecting boxes
and packing my things.
this apartment means living by someone else's watch

and waiting.

when i leave the city limits this time,   i leave behind the fear,
the rage.

i bring with me the trust i will spend
the next four months sewing back together

i am reservoir water saved for the last drought
so i move to the desert and wait for the sun
to dry me up.

TO THE FERNS ON THE INTERSTATE

it is reckless to abandon
these hot cups of yesterday:
home echos blue across the starlight,
it is august when i start to shiver.

and there it is, long and strange
the letting go
wonders of:

the ferns on the interstate:
socks under the bed, unwashed
hair, dirt clinging to fingernails.
gas station bathrooms where i try to clean
the sunspots from my hands.

to tell a story of abandon is to tell the story
of waking up in a new place, of
feeling the deep pressure
listlessly driving me again to the shoreline
of the desert. *i really want to,*
i just don't know how, i really want to,
i just don't know if i will want to
tomorrow.

here i am, again,
hounding for undergrown and overworn
freedom. solace in the salt. my thirst
only satisfied in dreamland.

THE DAYS I DON'T THINK ABOUT YOU

i think
there will never be
a day i don't think about
you. the yesterday
in me has been wandering
wild for 10 years now—
to make sense of the pain
is to define it in a language
nobody knows but everyone
understands. it is
a redefinition of childhood,
making all the pieces
west of fear. it is far
too early in this life
to be afraid of who i am
i have already spent too many
years wanting to shrink
when i was meaning
to grow; perhaps every woman
at one point makes this
mistake, for all these
eyes on me cannot be
what it feels like
to come home.

CRIME JUNKIE

after my car window was smashed
i started listening to crime podcasts
on my way to work, to find a story
that would make me feel okay
with my own life. i soon learned
my own safety does not come at the expense
of someone else's. now i am
sitting in the silence of a desert highway,
seconds away from scaring myself out of love.

SEVEN YEARS

i want to breathe it all in at once
the seven years i missed, here, in sedona
marked red by heat so hard i turn to stone –

if i am not full, i am emptying.

if i am not

moving, i am sinking. sick with the knowing
of what i missed but a luminescent sunrise
of what we could become. i don't want to be
known by the world, i want to know myself
and i want to learn to live
fearlessly, like you, with urgency so calm
it spends afternoons in the shadow of a waning sun.
your approach to waking up is to ask why you slept,
what the pause gave to you. instead,
i move from the moments too quickly, the fear
they will turn sour, they will start to cry before
i have time to run.

EXPECTATIONS OF JOY

leaving
the state
of be—
—ing, we
cross the
border
and some
how it
is still
raining.
 i had
expec—
—ted for
my bones
to be—
—come you
and for
sunshine
to be
the thirst
of all
rivers
west of
Sedona.

WHAT YOU TOOK FROM ME (PART 1)

what you took from me was not
my two week's worth of cash tips
or my annual national park pass.

what i lost comes back in
pieces.

see, there are things they took
that i didn't even realize were gone
until i was handing the park ranger
my empty palm and checking
my mailbox twice a day
until my new ID arrives.

i like to say i have no attachment
to material objects, *butcher skin*
embroidery thread of every color
braided to one, and i have never loved anything
more than the safety in your eyes.
this grieving is voluntary
but beneath bed sheets, it is real;
i am terrified of what yesterday
i saw as certain

these days of doubt, you are more than
one country away. i gave too much
weight to the phone screen, believing
safety to always be assumed. i took it
for granted, when i called 911
i was put on hold and then told

[this is not an emergency.]

when, that week, i stopped sleeping through someone else's night:

i told myself   *this is not an emergency*

when i barricaded my door with two locks
a laundry basket and my kitchen chair

i told myself

                                    this is not an emergency

it was simple enough to name
what it was *not*, but not as easy
to name what it was.

the police said   *this was not a violent crime*

because there was no blood and i was not there

and the difference between what you said

                                    that must have felt so violating

and what she said

                                    that really sucks

was so clear i cried at both.
i cried in the grocery store and the back room at work
because when the car window was fixed
and the credit cards were new in my pocket,
the glassy parts of my life still felt broken.

and i could not fix what i could not understand.
so i wrote what was stuck free, every story ending
in the princess gets the bride, no, the princess finds

the groom dead and swims across the lake
to find the place where she can count all her fingers and toes
to ensure she has not left her body, just the trauma.

I WOULD HAVE DONE IT

what is more draining than being told
you need to get out of your head.

because,
      if i knew how to break through this

of course i would have done it.

THERE IS MORE THAN THIS

how can i tell you
there is more than this?
you have been living
with one eye drawn
distinctively shut.
even now i can
only feel this newness
as it comes in waves.
i need you
like i need the rain
to know what the sun
feels like. this coin flip
of getting better
and the losing you
lands every penny
in the bottom
of a foggy fountain.
i will not jump in,
and i will not drag you out.
i want to know more
about you than i know
about myself;
the world goes to sleep
thinking about how
you think about me.
there is more than this,
girl. how many days
will have to go by
before you say my name?

WHAT YOU TOOK FROM ME (PART 2)

i relive the moment my identity was taken from my
car's front passenger seat so many times
i see myself as the person who smashed the window.

i think of my laptop, with the bear-shaped sticker
of pikes peak, and wonder whose hands it is in.
i imagine they have scraped off the stickers
with the sharp end of a box cutter,
sold it for $100 out of a parking garage bathroom.
they don't need to erase the joy from it - i have done that already.

three and a half week's worth of research notes are gone
as are at least two dozen poems and
a decades worth of pictures.

i don't mind this loss, not entirely.
the only form of identification i want back
is my passport
so i can leave.

THE UNBECOMING

i have made this inspiration my entire being; my earth.

and the beauty in its stillness is uncompromising
      and wild, this existence,
      fire bound and stuck

i will write the wonder out of this
if i keep my head bent and wandering,
it is the focus in the pause i lack,

                    i cannot

wait until this feels like water again
desert sunrise and hunger keeps me motionless
against a bluing sky,

            feeling every joy there is

in stubbing my toe on the root of a cactus, flowering,
i say *i have not written anything worth reading
since last summe*r, july, when it pooled in my entire breath,

scabbed against my way of breathing. but i am learning
the way soil will scream its way to the surface
until desire runs it hot and dry

under the piercing sun of noon. i am learning
to write this country real until it begs to be forgotten,
to pull apart the edges is to destroy, willingly;

this is the unbecoming.

THE SCREAM OF A SIREN

concrete cabinetry, the scream of a siren from chiseled lips,
the feeling of being stuck, an impeachment of self.
the design of my skin contorted
to a confinement of the mind.
they say this hormonal edging of love will dissipate
but the bleeding of sunglasses to eyesight
never lets me see what is real, no matter how many times
i try to find the meaning. as if
concussed is confused, because it is here
where now i cannot leave.

find it. i dare to you define this and wait
as the granite melts with snow in the summer.

YESTERDAY'S LEFTOVERS

i am frozen in the light of the fridge, the remembering
salting me cold, the wanting to wrap myself tighter around this
hardens itself to doubt. it will not be. yesterday is

the part leftover, the brain dump, the dream circle,
the place where my body intersects with the moon,
the moment time becomes a cottage in southern maine;
rain is a memory i can only recall the smell of.

the yesterday is the place i could hope on, where nothing
looks as bright as what was once an inside out rainbow,
thoughts as strings, as feathers, as leaves, as air and breath and
the willingness to think of it all again today.

OPPORTUNITIES

opportunities come to me in sea glass
broken into stilts like wildfire clouds
on a mountain ridgeline, backbone
bent from age and weather.

I THINK IT IS RAINING TODAY

i think it is raining today, though i cannot tell;
my shades are closed, my windowsill bare –
scared of what would happen to the plants without the sun
and here, i promised you i would keep it all alive

my room becomes a mirror image of my body
where everything is harder to pick up
in the nighttime because everything seems
like day, illuminating and visible, too clear
to not try to see through

i think it is raining today, and i am happier
than even the thirst of the trees; i feed myself
the water, tell my body
this will never be your fault.

TO A COFFEE SHOP IN SEATTLE, WASHINGTON

the first time i heard myself say, *i'm from colorado*
it was like blinking my eyes open
on the first day of spring, sun still timid,
but more awake than i ever thought possible.

four years ago, i was a mix of city-state-forest-mountain.
i was scrambling landscapes like pencil shavings,
digging the earth from beneath me;

kicking sidewalk soda cans into the gutter,
i wished for trees. i stayed away wondering
what it would feel like, to be in the dirt again,
knowing i chose to sleep in the same bed
every night, the day i dared to make a single space
look more like a home than my own body.

you are van rides in the pitch black,
taunting the pavement to be just light
enough to see our footsteps, the high top
chuck taylors running through
wet morning grass.

to that coffeeshop in seattle, washington:
i am blue and homesick.

SUMMER, 2019

the first day
i stuck to my notes, read
what was already written,
and slept in the backseat
of a 1998 toyota camry

i left paper scraps between the sheets
of every bed i have laid in this summer,
so far i am a sharpie-bled book, never knowing
what it should look like, pink.

and i like to think of it like this:
summertime but speechless,
silent and heavy with sun.
just barely breathable.

(RE)CONNECTION

i lost the curve of my bones
on new hampshire's wood-worn paths,
sharpened by pine and pennies, i ran. years and miles   later
you caught butterflies on your tongue
and carried them to meet my healing scabs
willing the warmth back, you brought me   sun,
gave me the north star to travel with me   west,
here you left me the aching,
a reminder that what i left was not what i lost
                i cried and still, i am not the sadness.
                at some point, i stopped running and it did not end me.

VISTA: 50 FEET AHEAD

how do i make this more than
just another view, another vista,
another pullout from the road
to take a picture of the sunset
in my rearview mirror?

i aspire to make the mundane special
tuesday is magic if you let it
i will not get so used to the joy
that i cannot feel it throughout every turn

stability seems like a good idea, so
i will have to let myself get full(er) than this.

I HAVE NEVER KNOWN BEAUTY LIKE THIS

the first time she visited my family in massachusetts,

she said to me

i am so proud of you.

she said to me

you are not your family. you do not have to become
this; you can grow out.

and when my mother saw the ways i did not need her anymore

    it was like falling
    one hundred feet
    waiting for the ground
    to catch me

it was like the last pencil point
that piece of yellow wood will ever have

    it was like the first day of kindergarten,
and
    the day the carseat was removed from the backseat

it was the day i started to weigh enough to set off the airbag.

when the fear
was made real.   what made me safe would also hurt,
and i never knew
how much.

she held me and let her warmth be mine too.
                                        she held me
and answered all the questions i had but would never ask.

she wasn't afraid to touch my skin and wake me.

                                        she said
you are not fragile, you are not weak,
but treated me like a piece of sea glass,
too special to risk breaking. i have never had
this.

she was taller than me
        but would never stand up straight enough to show it.
she taught me to love

        the parts of my body that protected
        me from myself
        the me that was lightened
        and floating
        too scared to touch the ground
        for longer than a moment,

i fear this joy will be used up, fear that it will stay
and i will not see it as joy, because i see it
in everything.

i have never known beauty before i met her.

EVERYTHING WILL BE ALRIGHT

this puddle looks at itself like it is an ocean;
it can feel so big to watch yourself grow with rain,

what if our roots grew from weather, not wine?
what if we learned to speak so softly to one another
our breath was air and we knew what it said?

kindness cuts holes in the loneliness, though
it is unpredictable – how do i know
which flower pots will bloom? you are
glued to the seasons with dirt and mulch
letting fertilizer nurture you back to the ground,
swear that
                    everything will be alright

but goodness is subjective, love is not.

sunset

finality, transition

DEAR SEDONA

this morning i am falling apart
at the thought of leaving.
i am idling,
looking for reasons to stay,
telling myself *maybe tomorrow*
it will feel easier
everything i want comes to me
in fresh banana bread
and a day too hot to breathe by 9 am. heat
drives me restless, a wanting
to understand finally not wanting
to run. i want to stay here today. every moment i find
more of this city to love, more dirt
i have never seen before. i have found
faith in believing
i am exactly where i need to be
dreaming reality to *it will all work out*
if i just stay in this canyon, if i let
this red rock read my bones in yesterday's language
every word i don't understand i still want
to know. here i am
beginning to trust, believing
life can be beautiful again.

STAY WILD, FLOWER CHILD

stay wild, flower child
bread tags on the rim of a sweat-stained
bucket hat, color undisturbed
and rooted to waterless colorado soil
the stream of sun through heavy morning smoke
here i am: pink with warmth.

...

stay wild, flower child, you are etchings
on an old t-shirt; for weeks i have not known
the day, or the time, or the heat, but i know
how it feels to live and breathe
the beginning and end of each day, there are cycles
to this that i cannot see when all i hear is
the plunge of an ice scoop and the smell of grease,
hot in the afternoon. air conditioning coiled
around prickled skin, here is where my body learned
to adjust to the senses and the seasons,
and never feared what made me feel alive.

...

stay wild, flower child
you will move to the second largest city
in colorado and claim it to be a small town legacy
the whiff of hot city smells buckled against mountains
there are enough woods here to believe
every stop sign is the trailhead i park my bike at
and each morning is honeysuckling
car exhaust and coffee beans. **there is
wonder in the familiar, but there is joy
in what appears to be new.**

...

stay wild, flower child, your letters
are drawn in sun-silk ink, believing to be
the time capsule unimagined and dreams
of the childhood left behind, the place
where pavement curled with weeds and ferns
became one with the woods and the rain.
that town had a single gas station and
a long walk to school. roots are built to last
and weave themselves to trees; wonder is found
in moss. there are so many similarities
between desert and flood, drought and
new beginnings.

...

stay wild, flower child, you learned to read the stars
without the guide book; that summer you saw
patterns in the plaid of the sky, make
every cloud a home and every leaf a blanket.
i fall asleep to the words
of the one letter i got this summer. now, i am not afraid
to sleep in the pitch black
of a mountain night.

—

I AM WRITING LOVE POEMS, TO PLACES

i thought i could undo what we had become
just by getting the combination right,
a twisted ankle with a diary lock
crumpled in paper by the heel.

how silly to think:
here i am, sitting by the creek
in moab, writing love poems
to all the place i have gone
this year. how my first heartbreak
was utah august heat–this is when
i clawed my way through sand
to see the desert clearly, and
when i carried my tears, so
misty i could not
see any rock at all.

how silly to think: i am writing
love poems, to places.

I CANNOT BE ENTIRELY STONE

i have to start believing the world can be good
and kind, and real again. i cannot be
entirely stone, and the crumbling of my costume
requires peeling the paint layers back to paper
but not setting fire to what is dry
                              there is a fire ban and i will follow the rules, like

i used to be
fearless with the flame, edging my hands
towards their embers to feel where the heat
comes from. but now we are the closeout sale
of the fireworks shop in new hampshire, buying even
what we don't want just because it is cheap.
it is a sunday when i realize

        i don't want to keep selling my words
        or my hands. i don't want to advertise
        the everything i have become.

LOVE LETTERS TO YESTERDAY

life is asking me, quietly, to see
that *six years ago i was too close*
to where i am today. yet an abundance
has changed, beyond what the writing tells
and i am reflection in the pool
of my eyes, an emulation of stars
that bleed memories on colder days.

the places where i start
are always taut and lovely
and somewhere between consciousness
and imagination. *nothing* lies
more than pictures, smiling
for the photo is not smiling
in the photo. these are the things
i tell myself when,

yesterday bleeds the border yellow
but still the bright orange of sunrise;
some days are just as vibrant
as highlighter scratches
on the back of an index card,
the joy found before time
looked like time meant;
climbing trees late
into the afternoon, loving
the lack of responsibility i would someday
inherit, living on simplicity
and after-school ice cream cones.

parts of me don't want to hear
the poems i write about the years

after this, all the disqualifications of
well, we had enough money or
i had both my parents or
i was given opportunities

but opportunities don't look like
opportunities when they are spray-painted
a transparent coat of guilt, of
this is what you got, this what you have
to return.

i send love letters to yesterday, to the me
who thought my own hardship depended
on someone else's judgment, that maybe
my worst day was better, but girl,
the hurt still hurts and you can't
think yourself out of that one.

PATTERNS

when it is just you and the soil
my freckles are the constellations
before the sun sets.

                i create their patterns, mimic.

i see the sky's stars brighter in their absence.
and there is nothing about this
that does not scare me.

everything exists in the house
between dinner and dusk,
when it is still light enough to see
the dirt stains on my palms and knees
all my body's imperfections
undergrown and too warm
to survive this winter.

N.H.

driving along the coast until the wind moves us inward
to this little rustic town on the way to maine –
eyeglasses fog from salt off the sea

new hampshire looks like deer tracks at the base of a tree,
pine, or maple, or the lighthouse lamp oil
off the portsmouth shore,

                              only those who got out
will ever write about these cobbled streets, as,
this is not boston, no city lights under april
rainfall, storefronts of gold beaded bracelets

                                              this is
woods until you reach the sea, gas station coffee
at the bottom of cobleigh hill road, being
the single car at a four-way stop,

places here, in these illustrated forests,

they are underwritten
so i am giving them words, the way

i keep the small town cold in my pocket,
whatever desert i sleep in tonight, i can still
smell what it feels like
                              if i want to go home.

WHO KNEW THE WIND
COULD CARRY SUCH HEA(R)T

who knew the wind could carry such heat
discomfort evolves in frustration
angry is the inevitable and unrefined

and what the heat brings out in me
is a desert of my own. i am defiled by
each itch the wind procures
                              sometimes,
                              i forget that it has turned to night, sometimes,
                              i forget to say good morning to the moon

so here i am, pleading for the sun to go
a promise to make comfort in the cold
until it turns to beauty.

in an instant, i am overcome with wonder;
there is suddenly no more desire to cleanse
the organic to its plastic companion, there is nothing
that could make me want to stay more than
the thought
                i can still love what i cannot control.

when i am this far from my skin,
i run to the ocean that raised me, forever thirsty
for love's salty tongue.
what the desert in my bones hopes for
is the moon's last lung and the earth's
first heartbeat. to try to understand this
is to let heat between my legs
and teach it to live. with just womanhood

i can birth myself an atheist bible
where every line leads me back
to morning-born shrubs and sun-hung smiles.

chapped lips, cuts on fingertips
the smell of sweat and the ache of unwashed hair
the obsession with water rises again – and i am
returning myself to the sea.

here: you and me on the rock
the minutes pass with a recognition
of silence, the state of being
static but modifying
in its own ethereal way.

just like all the stars in the sky, my eyes can't comprehend
these rocks are moving too, dancing with their own rhythm
and it is slow – so slow generations pass
without seeing a single sidestep. they are

cliffs strung like taffy, tough
against the colorado river
and when i see a car climbing its rim,
the headlights draw me back to longing.

i shift myself to the mind; if i were here alone...
i would have spent hours
staring at the same rock
willing the poetry out of me
like it was something already written.

i would think of how i would say this to you
in a series of short breaths and syllables
or one long tone of love

how would i have told you
all these feelings
without you here, too? it is everything

to look up from my notebook
see past, present, and future
in one long line of living
when i say

                i do not have anything
                to write about

it is because i do not remember
what it felt like to hold your hand

say goodnight to the desert

                        this is the shifting
                        to dark

the letting go of the fear.

ON MY THIRD DAY IN SEDONA

on my third day in sedona,
i fell in love with the iced coffee
at layla's bakery and cafe.

we climbed red rocks
until the sun ran us away,
heat shook us to shade

and you made every morning
look like it had just been born.

i cried at the thought of leaving.

just like before, the healing
i have found only comes in the road
and every one leads here. how can i
claim to know this life
i see for myself, for it is
just a mirror of where i am.

and you, sedona, are too curious
to avoid, too bright to be forgotten,
too full of life for these stars of yours
to ever burn out.

RIVER SONG (PART 2)

my fourth day at the river
i camp so close to a tree
i can smell its sap

i do not remember
what the forest felt like
before it was green.

i can
almost recall what the desert
tasted like at sundown.

and

i am in love with how it feels
to be cold under the moon.

QUESTIONING THE QUIET MIND

you spent all of yesterday
thinking of nothing – yes,
it has been wonderful.

WHY I CAN'T WRITE WITH YOU BESIDE ME

because my words will becomes
your words, or yours
will become mine.
                    i have not yet
learned to write well without
giving in to a little bit to the sadness
because it was where my words were born.
there will always be my whisper of doubt
between these broken ribs of poetry, as if
every line will end in a question,
                                        of
how am i going to tell this truth tomorrow,
even more than today?

FEET FIRST

i stopped and swung the canyon
feet first through the fear

      these are all the things i do not want to do.

not quite the kind of dread mustered
from sitting cross-legged at the river
as the sun rises, the approaching heat
terror unbound by vortex energy;
all the ways i have not yet learned to feel.

it is the first day i decided not to fight back.
i was lightened by consciousness,
the earliest meadow
but i do not know what to do
if i am not pushing you away.

i do not want to tell you how this feels
in my body, why can't i give you
cain's analogy so you will wake up knowing
the ache is catapulting everywhere
but it is always, mostly, in my chest.

NATURE POETRY ON SAD DAYS

i get tired of writing nature poems
for a world that does not always love me back

COFFEE SHOP CONVERSATIONS
Flagstaff, Arizona

backwards of belonging, this coffee shop
lingers long after the 6pm close,

the patio remains open and collects stories,
leans against the depth of decaf,
the dust and debris of what cannot be caffeinated.

these conversations that happen with empty glasses
would not change my unbecoming, anyways.

here, the sun is still wild on cherry blossoms
and huddles in community with the aspen trees.

i left my job because i was beginning to know

the capitalistic community
better than my own, saying

i will never work the 9 to 5 yet
here i am counting the hours

til the sun sets, minutes belong
to the timesheet, joy becomes dull

even on payday.

so i have written my two weeks notice

but i can't help to think that today
maybe i should stay for one more closing shift

the desert is a woman too

to see what the patio has to say
about all this wonder.

SORE CITY

i think that a palace can be tired
of being, of staying, of changing.

sore from the seasons.

this town could be
one i find erased from a map one day,
well-rested and smiling from *no more yearning*
or performing.

the face of this city
has muscles that never sleep, in fact
they have never even tried to, if it is
all you know,
you will live tired
until it runs you off the map.

SOUTHBOUND

as to write in only directions,
left to directing to a place that may be just
a settling of the stomach, a knot undone,
singeing the edges of that paracord
and braiding yourself into the highway,
like another right turn is just the right exit,
these numbers
reverse when they want. they don't. make sense,
i mean. state highway 133, forty
minutes southwest, winding yourself,
a hammock strap around a tree, a jack-in-the-box
ready for the school zone speed limit,
for any sign different. thinking ten
hours isn't so long if you drive too fast,
but let the fear of running a stop sign
slow you down. learn to love the yellow light
here. in new mexico, a strawberry smoothie
is a milkshake with whipped cream and no straw.
empty sidewalks on my way home to a ghost town,
diners and gas stations are just divots and hiccups
of the road. so i write myself another way, a reminder
that self is sane and tomorrow is a lonely drive
back. reverse the reverse. tomorrow will be that unwinding
of everything unwound too soon. forget that.
turn down cimarron st, find yourself across
state lines, still driving south.

OAK CREEK

by the time i leave
                    it is 4:30 and the sun
has already sank beneath
                    the canyon walls.

what was brilliant light has become
                    shade. in this river i found
time pause, the current
                    charged and excited, the evening
lingering.

it is the night of tarantula hunting
                    and moon healing,
laughter across a field
                    empty through june.

YESTERDAY'S REARVIEW MIRROR

i saw tomorrow in yesterday's rearview mirror.
i don't know what to do with the polaroid, so i leave it out
to bleach white from the exposure of a passionate sun.
you told me there was so much more, and i believed you,
and every morning i tried to see how this rising was different
than the day before, and i fell into even more bloodlust
by the desire to unbecome. tonight, i have decided to sit on this patio.
under the weeds grow the flowers in the sidewalk cracks;
there has to be a time we will start to think of the useless
as the most beautiful points of tension to have ever existed.

THE ECONOMY OF NATURE

you are driving to the canyon's edge
teaching a tree to grow from sun-hard dirt
and paying yourself in leaves

the economy of nature is well-earned
and never spent.

MOVEMENT ON SHAKY LEGS

                  the writing in me fears
i will have nothing left to write about.
                  the writing in me fears
i am living the same day
for three weeks. now, new memories
only come to me in halves.
                  the writing in me fears
                  desire
because it looks like running, barefoot on pavement,
pen ink drying under the desert sun. i call this:
movement
       on
            shaky
               legs.

BEAUTY COMES TO ME (IN SECONDS)

beauty comes to me
in seconds, the visitation
of a place taut against
the ability to relive the first time

the second time, i swear
i will love it more. what i remember
                              i remember
with age; three mysteries
too many for my explanation
of how it all worked out
for me to be here again.

this is the process of blind being:
driving without knowing the destination, yet

that it something i would never imagine doing.

in fact, i plan with such purpose
that three years from now i will have seen
every inch of this park, as long as
the months tell stories in cycles
and every time we get to the beginning
i am *here*,

for the second time.

THIS CANNOT BE MY LIFE, IT IS MY DREAM

i have tried for three months now
to not fear the heat
to be able to say to the sky
it is 110 degress and that is the least terrifying thing
of this entire day.

arizona brings me to every show's ending,
i am dreaming of her name
in the line of credits. there
are a thousand ways to say i love you
to sedona.

this is the final sunset,
and when i drive in reverse
the wrong way down a dead end road
i see it, clearly:

this cannot be my life, for it is my dream.
what makes a dream a dream is that
it has not happened yet.

The Desert is a Woman Too

a poetry collection

GIRL GROWTH
While this poem does reference womanhood and girlhood in many different ways, I want to expand the meaning and use of "girl" to extend beyond just female-identifying people. For the readers who do not identify as a woman, let this be the invitation for you to find your own identity within this poem.

DAYDREAMS
Don't be afraid to ask for help.

THE WAY EVERYTHING IS SUPPOSED TO GO
Written in the Grand Canyon in April 2023.

LEARNING TO READ A COMPASS
This is a poem that has experienced so many things in its evolution. Originally written pre-pandemic, I rewrote much of this after more of my road trip adventures out west. I think of this poem as a mix of all the lovely and terrifying things about leaving and letting go of the place I grew up in.

WINTER IN NEW HAMPSHIRE
Written in absolute and distinguished disconnection from the theme of heat and desert throughout this entire collection, this poem, in particular, is a reminder that conflicting things can actually be surprisingly similar.

OUT OF SORTS
Written in Bryce Canyon National Park.

ONLY DEAD FISH SWIM WITH THE CURRENT
For many months of 2023, "only dead fish swim with the current" was a mantra that reminded me to push myself to be the best version of me. This poem also references d.s.b poetry's chapbook *We Were Fire in the Night*, which is placed in the line "we are meant to be fire in the night." I have been deeply inspired by Matt's work, and am honored to include this line in my poetry.

THE SCREAM OF A SIREN
One of my very close friends is also a poet. He has helped me find flexibility in the way that I write. This poem was created during one of our writing sessions, where we gave each other 10 words to include in a poem and 5 minutes to write.

This is an exercise that has helped me break away from using the same words over and over, and pulls me out of writer's block when I desperately need it. I am beyond grateful to have Finn, who I dedicate this poem to.

THERE IS MORE THAN THIS
Many of these poems, this one included, are letters to myself that I hope can extend to you, the reader.

YESTERDAY'S LEFTOVERS
The line "what once was an inside out rainbow" directly references Amelie Honeysuckle's book *What Once Was An Inside Out Rainbow*.

WHY KNEW THE WIND COULD CARRY SUCH HEA(R)T
"The smell of sweat and the ache of unwashed hair" is from my first book, *as if to return myself to the sea*.

CRIME JUNKIE
This poem refers to the podcast "Crime Junkie."

(RE)CONNECTION
A poem dedicated to my best friend, Grace Gray.

NATURE POETRY ON SAD DAYS
Although no, the world will not always be kind, nature has given me more than I could have ever imagined.

acknowledgments

It is a great privilege and joy to extend a long and loving thank you to Indie Earth Publishing for the endless patience and creative freedom they have given to me throughout the process of publication and bringing my book to life. More specifically, I want to thank my incredible editor and cover artist, Flor Ana, for her dedication and passion to all aspects of poetry.

I have been continually surprised by the wonder and inspiration that others around me have produced in order for me to complete this poetry collection. I offer a huge thank you to my amazing partner, Lila, who has not for a single second stopped believing in me, and to my family in Massachusetts, who respond to all my ambition with unwavering support.

The year of 2023 in which this poetry collection was created was one of healing, growth, challenge, and joy. I owe much of this to two people I am proud to call some of my closest friends. Grace Ann and Holly, thank you for your constant and powerful support through this process and so much more. And Kendall Hope, thank you for your positivity that never fails to remind me of the wonderful things in life.

Thank you to the Colorado College English Department, who awarded me the Colorado College Grants in Writing which allowed me to spend the summer in the desert, writing this book! The incredible opportunities I have been given as a student studying creative writing have massively impacted my ability to dedicate the time to complete two full-length poetry collections. I am beyond thankful for the professors, classes, and other educational influences that have helped me find the time and place for my writing.

It is impossible to ignore the presence and influence of the natural world in this collection of poetry. I have endless gratitude for the landscapes that have helped me write these poems. To the desert: thank you.

Kristen Richards is the author of the poetry collection *as if to return myself to the sea*, released in August 2023 by Indie Earth Publishing. Her work has previously been published in the Leviathan, The Elevation Review, and Flossy Lit Magazine, and her poem *(self)love notes* was also published in *GLOW: Self-Care Poetry for the Soul*. Kristen is an adventurous spirit by nature, and loves exploring the mountains of Colorado and deserts of Arizona and Utah. *The Desert is a Woman Too* is her second full-length poetry collection.

Connect with Kristen on Instagram:

@kristenrichardspoetry